SOME FACTORS AFFECTING RESUMPTION OF INTERRUPTED ACTIVITIES BY PRESCHOOL CHILDREN

UNIVERSITY OF MINNESOTA
THE INSTITUTE OF CHILD WELFARE
MONOGRAPH SERIES NO. XVI

Some Factors Affecting
Resumption of Interrupted Activities
by Preschool Children

BY

EVELYN KATZ, Ph. D.

DIRECTOR OF STUDENT PERSONNEL, CLEVELAND COLLEGE, AND
ASSOCIATE IN PSYCHOLOGY, DEVELOPMENTAL HEALTH INQUIRY,
MEDICAL SCHOOL, WESTERN RESERVE UNIVERSITY

GREENWOOD PRESS, PUBLISHERS
WESTPORT, CONNECTICUT

Library of Congress Cataloging in Publication Data

Katz, Evelyn.
    Some factors affecting resumption of interrupted
activities by preschool children.

    Reprint of the ed. published by University of
Minnesota Press, Minneapolis, which was issued as
no. 16 of University of Minnesota, Institute of Child
Welfare Monograph series.
    Bibliography: p.
    Includes index.
    1. Motivation (Psychology) 2. Child study.
I. Title. II. Series: Minnesota. University.
Institute of Child Development and Welfare.
Monograph series ; no. 16.
BF723.M56K37 1975   155.4'23   75-12944
ISBN 0-8371-8081-3

Originally published in 1938 by the University of
Minnesota Press, Minneapolis

Reprinted with the permission of University
of Minnesota Press

Reprinted in 1975 by Greenwood Press, Inc.,
51 Riverside Avenue, Westport, Conn. 06880

Library of Congress catalog card number 75-12944
ISBN 0-8371-8081-3

Printed in the United States of America

10 9 8 7 6 5 4 3 2

FOREWORD

Among the several studies arising out of the personality theories of Lewin, the present monograph deserves particular commendation for its analytical and critical approach and for the clarity of its style. Basing her investigation of the resumption of uncompleted activities on the studies carried out by Lewin and his students, particularly Ovsiankina, Miss Katz worked out an experiment, with a homogeneous group of children as subjects, through which she has been able to make several additions to our knowledge of "tension systems" and their relation to overt behavior. Her investigation presents at least partial answers to some fundamental questions that previous studies of the same problems have failed to answer, especially the question of the extent to which the presence or absence of other activities in the environment affects resumption of an interrupted activity. Both her quantitative and qualitative findings, presented in a terse and logical manner, are useful contributions to the exploration of this very interesting field.

JOHN E. ANDERSON
Director, Institute of Child Welfare
University of Minnesota

ACKNOWLEDGMENTS

The author wishes to express her gratitude to the many persons who helped to make this investigation possible: to Dr. Florence L. Goodenough for directing the experiment; to numerous principals and teachers of nursery schools, kindergartens, etc., for their willing cooperation in furnishing subjects; to Evelyn Raskin for her helpful suggestions in the preparation of the manuscript; and to Ruth Rippner for helping to obtain subjects.

E. K.

CONTENTS

SOME FACTORS AFFECTING RESUMPTION OF INTERRUPTED ACTIVITIES BY PRESCHOOL CHILDREN

I. INTRODUCTION AND REVIEW OF THE LITERATURE

The Problem

The impetus for the formulation of the problem under investigation was provided by the theoretical system of Kurt Lewin, who attempts to develop a theory of personality by advancing a series of "dynamic laws in the field of needs and emotions." One of these basic laws holds that when an activity is begun a tension system is set up within the individual and that this tension system is discharged when the goal of the activity is reached. The law is based partially on the findings of several investigations which show that if an individual is interrupted during the carrying out of an activity, he tends to resume that activity at the earliest opportunity.

In the experimental study of the influence of various factors upon the frequency of resumption, the following factors have been considered significant enough to warrant investigation: the nature of the task, the type of interruption, the phase of the task during which interruption occurs, the length of the interruption, and the effect of a substitute activity. In a survey of the literature on this topic, however, the writer has found no attempt to set up an experiment that would leave the subject free after the interruption to choose between the interrupted task and a new activity. In the absence of such an opportunity to pursue another activity, it is quite conceivable that the resumption may indicate merely the need of the organism for activity of some sort, rather than a tendency to discharge the specific tension system corresponding to the interrupted task. In some of the experiments, to be sure, other tasks than the original interrupted one were present, but in every case these tasks had already been completed, and would probably have lost their interest value for the individual. If, however, it can be shown experimentally that, even when the subject is given an opportunity to engage in another interesting task, he chooses to complete the original interrupted one, then the concept of a specific tension system becomes tenable.

The present experiment attempts to investigate this aspect of the problem by determining the effect of the presence of other activities upon the frequency of resumption of an interrupted activity. More specifically, if, after interruption, the individual has an opportunity to choose between resuming the interrupted activity and engaging in a new activity, are the chances of his resumption as great as when no alternative activity is present? And, if the choice is between the interrupted activity and two other activities, are his chances of resumption as great as when no other activity is present or as great as when only one other activity is present?

A second question that this study seeks to answer is: Does the stage at which the task is interrupted affect the frequency of resumption? Ovsiankina (9) has found that the frequency of resumption is greatest when the subjects are interrupted at the beginning of a task, decreases for interruption near the middle, is lowest for interruption after the subjects have finished about three-fourths of the task, and shows a sudden rise when the interruption occurs near the end. She interprets these results to mean that a strong tension system arises at the beginning of an activity, that it decreases as the task progresses, and increases again as the task approaches completion.

If our results confirm Ovsiankina's finding that the frequency of resumption varies with the point of interruption, then a third question follows. Does the effect of the presence of an alternative activity upon resumption of the main activity depend in any way upon the stage of the task at which the interruption occurs?

The fourth question investigated may be stated thus: Does the frequency of resumption vary with the nature of the activity? Again it is necessary to cite the work of Ovsiankina, who found that certain types of tasks were resumed more frequently than others.

A fifth question, subsidiary to the main problems outlined above, is whether there is any difference in the frequency of resumption between groups of subjects varying in intelligence. Lewin (4, page 185) reports an unpublished study by Köpke and Zeigarnik in which it was found that the feeble-minded tend to resume interrupted activities more frequently than normal persons. In the present investigation we are concerned only with possible differences within the range of normal intelligence.

Lastly, we have inquired: Do groups of children from widely separated socio-economic classes differ in their tendency to resume interrupted activities?

It may be added that the investigator has been concerned not alone with arriving at answers to the foregoing questions, framed largely in quantitative terms, but has also attempted to observe and to interpret certain qualitative aspects of the behavior of individual subjects.

THE LITERATURE

A survey of the series of articles on uncompleted activities published in the *Psychologische Forschung* and edited by Kurt Lewin (6, 8, 9, 14) will give some indication of the factors previously investigated, of the methods of investigation, and of the results obtained. Of these experiments the one most closely related to the present study is that of Ovsiankina (9). Her subjects were 108 adults, mostly students, and 16 children between the ages of three and sixteen years. In general she employed the following technique. The subject was allowed to work at a task and was interrupted before he had completed it. After the period of interruption he was free to resume the interrupted activity if he desired. The fifteen tasks used in the experiment varied from activities with very definite goals, such as solving a puzzle, to those of a continuous nature, such as stringing beads when an unlimited supply of material was available. Interruption was accomplished in several ways: by giving the subject another task to perform, by specific instructions to cease work on the main task, by interrupting in such a way as to give the impression that the interruption occurred by chance, by asking the subject to introspect, and by diverting him through conversation. Results relevant to the present study may be summarized as follows:

1. Resistance to interruption was a typical phenomenon, which manifested itself by the subject's persisting in the main task, by his thinking of the main task during the interruption, and in several cases by his expressed resolve to complete the main task.

2. After the period of interruption the individual's behavior was characterized by a general tension, a feeling that there was something he had to do, without a clear recognition of the specific object producing this drive toward activity. Gradually, however, the impulse became more specific and was directed toward finishing the uncompleted task.

3. A 100 per cent resumption was found when the interruption occurred as if by chance, and only an 82 per cent resumption when the interruption appeared to the subject to be intentional.

4. The percentage of resumption was little affected by the duration of the interruption or by the fact that in some cases the interrupted task was in another room.

5. Resumption occurred more frequently when the task was interrupted at the beginning, middle, or end than when it was about three-fourths complete. It is concluded, therefore, that a high degree of tension exists at the beginning of a task, and that the tension decreases until just before the goal is reached. The nearness of the goal produces an increase in tension.

6. The interruption even of boring or unpleasant tasks was found to set up a quasi-need or tension system within the individual which was discharged by resumption of the activity.

7. When, after the interruption, the subjects were given an opportunity to work at tasks that they had completed and found interesting on a previous occasion but which they had not started before the interruption, only two out of nineteen subjects turned to them. Uncompleted tasks, even of an unpleasant nature, were frequently resumed, however. This finding points to the fact that it is the incompleteness of the task rather than its interest that is the stimulus for resumption.

8. A stronger tension system existed in those cases in which the intention to resume was present before the subject saw the unfinished work than in those cases in which the sight of the unfinished work led to resumption.

9. Very rarely did the sight of the unfinished work of another lead to a tendency on the subject's part to complete it.

10. The frequency of resumption was found to vary with the nature of the task. Tasks regarded by the subject as tests of his ability were resumed more often than tasks in which no problem existed for him. Tasks with definite goals showed a higher percentage of resumption than continuous tasks.

11. In a qualitative analysis of the data, Ovsiankina distinguishes among her subjects five different personality types and four different types of development of the tension system. She relates the types of tension system to the personality types and to the nature of the various tasks.

Another aspect of the problem was considered by Lissner (6), who investigated the discharge of needs or tensions through substitute activities. The hypothesis underlying her study is that, if the path to the original goal is blocked, the tension system can work itself out through a substitute activity, i. e., an activity related in some way to the main activity. The technique employed to investigate this hypothesis was to interrupt the main activity by a possible substitute task. After completion of the substitute task the subject was allowed 30 or 40 seconds (while the experimenter was busy writing a description of the behavior) in which he had an opportunity to resume the interrupted activity. It was assumed that if the interrupting task had substitute value, resumption of the original activity would be less frequent than if the task did not have substitute value. The substitute value of a substitute activity was computed by dividing the percentage of resumption occurring without a substitute activity by the percentage occurring with a substitute activity. The substitute activity was regarded as having substitute value if this quotient was larger than one; and the larger the quotient, the greater the substitute value. The main results of Lissner's investigation may be summarized as follows:

1. When no substitute activity was offered, resumption occurred in about 85 per cent of the cases, a percentage closely corresponding to that found by Ovsiankina.

2. In general, substitute tasks that were similar to the main task had a higher substitute value than dissimilar substitute activities.

3. Relatively easy tasks were shown to possess less substitute value than difficult ones. The difficulty of the task, however, was not so strong a factor in determining its substitute value as was its similarity to the main task, since similar easy tasks were found to possess greater substitute value than dissimilar difficult ones.

4. In general, the same substitute task possessed a lower substitute value for individuals who had set difficult goals for themselves than for those who had set relatively easy goals.

5. A substitute task involving a type of activity similar to that of the main task tended to possess a higher substitute value than a substitute activity in which the goal was the same as the main goal but in which the type of activity differed. When, for instance, the main task was modeling an animal out of plasticine, cutting the same animal out of colored paper possessed less substitute value than modeling a different animal out of plasticine. That is, the substitute value of a task depended upon whether, for the individual, a relationship existed between the main task and the substitute task.

The main theoretical conclusion drawn from the investigation is that the substitute value of a substitute task depends upon how closely the tension system corresponding to it is connected with the tension system corresponding to the main task. All degrees of relationship may exist between the two tension systems, from complete separation to a condition where the two systems are parts of one dynamic whole. Under the latter condition the discharge of one tension system leads to a discharge of the other. A substitute task similar to the main task ordinarily belongs to the same psychological field, and hence the tension system corresponding to it is likely to be dynamically connected with the tension system corresponding to the main task. It follows, then, that if the substitute task is similar to the main task, the discharge of its tension system will result in a discharge of the tension system corresponding to the main task, in which event the substitute activity acquires a high substitute value.

The purpose of Mahler's investigation (8) was to determine whether an unreal substitute activity can discharge a need or tension system. His subjects were 155 adults and 35 children. His procedure was to interrupt the subject when he had partly completed a task and to provide a substitute ending for the task. The substitute endings represented three degrees of reality. Substitution by doing, i. e., by overt action, was regarded as most real, substitution by thinking as least real, and substitution by talking as an intermediate degree of reality. Lissner's general technique was used.

The experiment with the group of children showed the substitute value for a substitute ending in the form of overt action to be 2.3 (quotient computed as in Lissner's experiment), while a substitute ending in the form of talking had a substitute value of only 1.2. For adults, too, the substitute value of doing was 2.2, as compared with 1.6 for that of talking. It was also shown that a substitute ending led to a tendency to resume more frequently than it did to actual resumption.

In general, doing had a higher substitute value than talking, but this relationship did not hold for certain tasks and for certain groups of subjects. In each case it is necessary to consider the relationship between the outer goal set by the experimenter and the inner goal set by the subject. For both adults and children, the frequency of resumption after a substitute ending was less when the task goal was reached by the substitute ending than when it was not. In the case of a problem task, the substitute ending had a high substitute value if the interruption occurred after the solution of the problem, but a low substitute value if the interruption came before solution of the problem.

In one experiment the subject was given an arithmetic problem to solve in writing. The substitute ending of talking led to resumption in only 17 per cent of the cases, as compared with 83 per cent resumption with no substitute ending. However, when the subject was told to think out the solution but not to tell the experimenter the answer or how he had arrived at it, resumption occurred in 100 per cent of the cases. The thesis that the solution of the problem is sufficient to bring about discharge of the tension system is contradicted by the fact that a new type of resumption appeared in these cases, usually taking the form of explaining the method of solution to the experimenter. From this behavior it was concluded that the solution is regarded as real, as a fact, only when it is brought into the social environment and receives recognition there.

When the subjects were instructed to think of a magical solution to the interrupted problem, resumption occurred in most cases. Such a fantastic substitute ending possesses little substitute value; however, in those cases in which the situation itself was of an unreal or fantastic nature, magical solutions gave higher substitute values.

Another series of investigations, less directly related to the present study than those reviewed above, tends to confirm the hypothesis that interrupted activities give rise to tension systems within the individual. In these experiments it is shown that uncompleted activities have a tendency to be better retained than completed ones. The most extensive work on this problem has been done by Zeigarnik (14). Each subject was given from eighteen to twenty-two simple tasks to perform and was told to finish them as well and as quickly as possible. Half of the tasks were completed by the subject, half were interrupted. The subjects were then asked to name the various tasks that they had performed. Zeigarnik found that uncompleted tasks were remembered almost twice as well as completed. The greater retention of the names of uncompleted tasks was not due to the shock effect of interruption, for similar results were obtained when the tasks that were to be completed were interrupted at some point before actual completion. Tasks interrupted near the middle or end were remembered better than tasks interrupted near the beginning. The explanation given for this difference is that the nearness of the goal brings an increased tension and also that by the end of the task the subject has put himself "into" the task more completely. Unfinished tasks with definite goals were recalled more frequently than so-called "continuous" tasks. In some cases tasks that were actually incomplete were completed "inwardly," i.e., they were regarded by the subject as completed and were recalled less often than "inwardly" incomplete tasks.

Schlote (13), Sandvoss (12), and Pachauri (10) repeated Zeigarnik's work, using nonsense syllables instead of meaningful memory material. In general their results substantiate Zeigarnik's findings. In an experiment with forty children, Rosenzweig (11) found that one group of children tended to recall finished tasks more frequently than unfinished, while another showed a greater tendency to recall the unfinished tasks. When the teacher rated these children on the trait of "pride" the former group had a higher average rating than the latter. A second investigation, in which adults were given jigsaw puzzles to put together, resulted in a greater frequency of recall of finished puzzles for the group that regarded the situation as a mental test, and a greater frequency of recall of unfinished puzzles for the group that believed they were helping the experimenter to classify the puzzles.

McKinney (7) departed from the type of investigation discussed above in that he was interested in determining, not whether the names of interrupted activities were recalled more readily than the names of completed activities, but whether the activity itself was better retained if it was uncompleted than if it was completed. Typical laboratory learning situations were used. One group of subjects (the experimental group) was instructed to learn a maze to three correct trials, while another group (the control group) was instructed to learn to one correct trial. The subjects in the former group were interrupted after one correct trial, thus leaving the task incomplete for them. The author concludes that "there were slight inconsistent tendencies in these experiments for the interrupted tasks to show greater retention." An experiment carried out in a similar manner, using words and nonsense syllables as learning materials, gave substantially the same results. The maze experiment was repeated, being interrupted when the errors had been reduced to one and again when the errors had been reduced to four. For the nonsense syllables the interruption occurred when the performance was at the one-error level. Retention was greater when the interruption came at the one-error performance than under any other conditions. Maze retention was more affected by interruption than was the retention of words and nonsense syllables. A cross-out test, used as the interrupting activity for the experimental groups and as the activity following completion of the task for the control groups, was affected in every case by interruption. The accuracy of the groups that were interrupted was below that of the groups that were allowed to complete the learning tasks.

An experiment of a radically different type was that of Freeman (2), who found that interruption of a mental or mental-muscular task caused an increase in muscular tension. His results also confirm the findings of other investigations that interrupted activities tend to be resumed. He differs, however, from other investigators in his interpretation of the phenomenon of resumption. He criticizes Lewin's concept of "psychic tensions," claiming that a simpler explanation can be given in terms of neuro-physiological processes. "The neural analogy of task resumption is the *competition* of rival impulses for a final common path. . . . The continuation of interrupted mental work involves not only reinforcement of the dominant response pattern, but also the reciprocal inhibition of irrelevant responses. In this struggle inhibition may take a form opposed to the interrupting response (resistance to interruption)."

In general one can say of the work that has come from Lewin's laboratory that it suggests problems rather than solves them. Brown (1) comments on Lewin's work in the following manner: "He is not yet able to set up his laws, but is simply in a position to show the material from which they must eventually come. His most important contribution is methodological rather than factual." If one accepts these limitations, there is little fault to find with the work. If, on the other hand, one regards the investigations from the point of view of the American laboratory psychologist, the deficiencies are numerous. As one instance, in his theoretical papers Lewin stresses the importance of the immediate environment in determining behavior. Yet in the reports of the experiments, there is an amazing lack of detail about the manner in which they were conducted. In Ovsiankina's investigation (9), for example, although the position and nature of objects other than the interrupted task would seem to be of some importance, in no part of the paper is any clear description given of the experimental situation. One of the photographs shows a subject seated before a table in a garden; from another part of the article one gets the impression that the experiments with the children were conducted inside the schools. Apparently the experimental situation was not the same for all of the subjects. Throughout, one looks in vain for the careful description of setup that is characteristic of American psychology.

Another criticism that may justly be made is that in many instances conclusions are drawn from too few cases. I do not wish to take issue here with Lewin's general tenet that one does not arrive at laws by multiplying cases and that events that occur once are as completely governed by laws as events that occur again and again. Nor am I opposed to the careful qualitative analysis of individual cases as a means of arriving at a knowledge of the dynamics of behavior. But such an emphasis does not carry with it any justification for drawing *quantitative* conclusions from an inadequate number of cases and without the use of adequate statistical techniques. Ovsiankina (9) concludes, for instance, that the tension system is strong at the beginning of a task, that it decreases gradually as the task progresses, and increases again at the end. This conclusion is based on the following data.

Point of Interruption	Number of Cases	Percentage of Resumption
After instructions	5	100
Beginning	32	92
Middle	142	84
Middle to end	45	72
End	97	83

The critical ratios for the differences between the percentages for the successive points of interruption are all less than 2, and hence any definite conclusions about the course of the tension system cannot be made on the basis of these data.

It is only just, however, to recognize that these experiments are of an exploratory nature and that their chief value is in suggesting problems and methods for more intensive research and research of a quantitative nature. The fact that they are technically short of perfection does not prevent them from serving as starting points for more carefully controlled studies. The present investigation is an attempt to answer fundamental questions that previous investigations of the same problem fail to answer. The extent to which the presence or absence of other activities in the environment affects resumption is obviously the most important problem, since in further investigations of interrupted activity it will be essential to know what parts of the physical environment influence the behavior of the individual with respect to the interrupted task.

II. THE EXPERIMENT

THE SUBJECTS

In the preliminary investigation 25 subjects between four and one-half years and five and one-half years were used. Thirteen of the children were in the kindergarten of the Institute of Child Welfare of the University of Minnesota and 12 were in the nursery school of a Minneapolis settlement house. The 25 children served as subjects in 65 experimental situations. In the main investigation 177 children of the same age range as those used in the preliminary investigation served as subjects for 486 experiments. Of these children, 146 were subjects in three experiments, 17 in two, and 14 in one. Nursery schools and prekindergartens of settlement houses provided 75 of the subjects; playgrounds, 39; public school kindergartens, 36; private nursery schools and kindergartens, 24; and acquaintances of the investigator, 3.

For the most part, previous investigators have used heterogeneous groups including both adults and children. The present writer used a group that was homogeneous as to age. She considered it more desirable to investigate the problem over a limited age range than to work with a heterogeneous group of subjects, since the effects of age on the behavior being investigated are unknown. Any conclusions that may be drawn will necessarily be limited to children of this age range. It is left to further research to determine whether age is a factor affecting behavior in these situations.

Children of kindergarten age were selected for several reasons. First, they are probably better subjects for this kind of experiment than school-age children, because their behavior is still quite spontaneous. The four- or five-year-old child regards situations of the type used as play, while the school-age child is more inclined to look upon such procedures as tests of his ability and upon the experimenter as a teacher. A second advantage to be gained from using subjects of this age is that it is fairly easy to plan activities that interest them. Lastly, they are more accessible than younger children, since they are more frequently found in nursery schools and kindergartens and on playgrounds.

The Tasks

Six occupations that were found in preliminary work to be of interest to children of kindergarten age were selected as the activities. They consisted of the following:

1. Mosaic

A model of a man constructed of 27 mosaic blocks one-half inch square was placed before the subject. He was given 27 duplicate blocks and was urged to make a man similar to the model by placing his blocks in the appropriate partitions of a box.

2. Matching Game

The subject was given a card on which were printed pictures of seven different fruits, with part of each picture cut out. Seven circular discs for completing the pictures were placed beside the card and the child was told to insert each disc into the picture that matched it. (See Figure 1.)

3. Christmas Tree

A Christmas tree cut out of green cardboard and containing 27 small holes was placed on the table before the child. He was given discs of different colors that fitted into the holes to represent lights, and was told that he might "decorate the tree with the lights."

4. Crayoning Balloons

Eight crayons and a sheet of manila paper on which were drawn seven

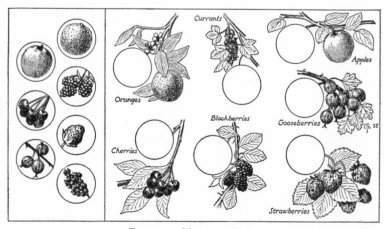

FIGURE 1.—Matching Game
Each of the seven discs at the left was to be inserted into
the picture matching it.

balloons were placed on the table. The child was told that he might crayon the balloons any colors he chose.

5. SEWING CARD

The child was given a piece of yarn and a card on which was printed a picture of a pail and shovel. He was then shown how to outline the pail and shovel by drawing yarn through the holes outlining the picture.

6. EASTER BASKET

The child was given an Easter basket cut out of green construction paper and pasted on a sheet of paper. Fifteen colored paper eggs were placed beside the basket and he was told he might paste them on the basket.

The following directions were used for the six tasks:

Mosaic. — "See, I have made a man out of some blocks" (pointing to model), "and I have given you some blocks so that you can make a man just like mine. We'll start by putting the head in here, like this." (Experimenter placed the head in the correct position.) "All right, now you may go ahead." If the subject had difficulty the experimenter helped him by showing him where to put the blocks.

Matching game.—"See all these pictures of different kinds of fruit? Part of each picture has been cut out. You must find the picture here" (pointing to discs) "that looks just like this one" (pointing to strawberry) "and put it in this hole, then find one that looks just like this" (blackberry) "and put it in this hole. Then do the rest just the same."

Christmas tree. — "Here are a lot of colored lights for the Christmas tree" (pointing to discs). "You may decorate the tree with the lights."

Crayoning balloons.—"Look at these circus balloons. I have given you all these crayons so that you may crayon the balloons any colors you like."

Sewing card.—"Here is a picture of a pail and shovel that we are going to sew. See, this is the way we do it." (Experimenter demonstrated with two holes and then allowed the child to continue.)

Easter basket. — "See this Easter basket. And here are a lot of eggs that you can paste on the basket. Paste them just the way you want them."

The interrupting tasks were five-piece puzzles constructed from pictures in the *Peter Rabbit* book. A picture of the completed puzzle was placed beside the puzzle pieces and the child was told, "If you put the pieces together you can make a picture just like that one." Three puzzles were used, one for each of the three situations to be described below.

Situation 1

Situation 2

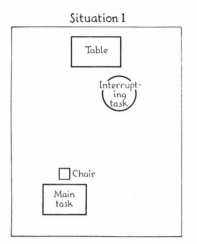
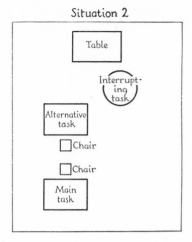

Situation 3

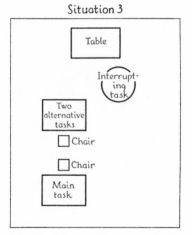

FIGURE 2.—PHYSICAL SETUP OF THE PRELIMINARY EXPERIMENT
In this arrangement the subject had to pass by the alternative
task to reach the interrupted main task.

CONDUCT OF THE EXPERIMENT

The preliminary investigation.—Figure 2 shows the physical setup of the experiment. In Situation I a kindergarten table and chair were placed four or five feet from the door. The main task was ready on this table when the child entered the room. In Situation II the main task was in the same position as in Situation I, and the alternative task was placed on a table four or five feet behind it. In Situation III the position of the tables was the same as in Situation II, the two alternative tasks being placed on the same table. In all three situations the materials not in use were kept on a table in the rear of the room and were covered so that the child could not see them. When a screen was available it was placed in front of this table.

In Situation I the experimenter brought the child into the room and showed him the task. "Come over here and look at this game that I brought for you to play with." When the child was seated at the table, the directions for performing the task were given. He was then allowed to work until he had completed about three-fourths of the task. For the various tasks, the interruption occurred at the following points:

Mosaic.—When 20 of the 27 blocks were inserted (74 per cent complete).

Matching game. — When 5 of the 7 discs were inserted (71 per cent complete).

Christmas tree. — When 19 of the 26 discs were inserted (73 per cent complete).

Crayoning balloons. — When 5 of the 7 balloons were crayoned (71 per cent complete).

Sewing card. — When 22 of the 30 holes were sewed (73 per cent complete).

Easter basket.—When 11 of the 15 eggs were pasted (73 per cent complete).

The child was interrupted in the following manner. The experimenter put the puzzle and the picture on the floor several feet from the subject and called him over. "Here is another game that I brought for you. It's a puzzle. Come here and look at it." If the child indicated, either verbally or by failure to stop working, that he intended to continue the task at which he was working, the experimenter took his hand and led him to the puzzle. He was then given instructions for solving the puzzle. To make the task easy the pieces were placed in the correct positions so that the child merely had to push them together to complete the puzzle. After the child had finished the interrupting task, which ordinarily required 30 to 60 seconds, the experimenter praised him and removed it. He was then told, "You may do anything you wish now and you may go back and play with the other children whenever you wish." In every case these directions led either to resumption of the interrupted task or to departure from the room.

In Situation II, two of the six tasks were used. When the child entered the room he was shown both tasks and was started at one of them. The same procedure was followed as in Situation I. After completion of the puzzle the child was free to do as he wished. He could complete the interrupted task, do the alternative task, or leave the room.

In Situation III, three of the six tasks were used. The child was shown the three tasks and was directed to work at one of them. The procedure was the same as that used in the other two situations. After he had completed the puzzle he was allowed to do any of the tasks that he wished and could leave the room at any time.

The main investigation.—The size and contents of the rooms used for the separate experiments varied considerably. This was unavoidable, since the experiments were carried out in settlement houses and in school buildings where it was necessary to use whatever space was available. In almost all cases, however, since the child had been in the room on previous occasions, its contents other than the experimental materials seemed to provoke little interest.

The setup of the main experiment is shown in Figure 3. For Situation I the arrangement of the materials was the same as in the preliminary experiment. The arrangement of the materials in Situations II and III of the preliminary experiment undoubtedly gave the alternative tasks an advantage over the main task, since after the interruption the alternative task or tasks were always nearer to the subject than the interrupted task and had to be passed before the subject could reach the latter. In the main investigation the table for the interrupted task and that for the alternative task were about three feet apart, and each was about seven or eight feet from the interrupting task. In Situation III the alternative tasks were placed on the same table in some of the experiments and on two different tables in others. When the experiments were conducted in schoolrooms, desks had to be used instead of tables. One desk was usually too small to hold two tasks, so three were used for the entire setup. The tables or desks were also placed about three feet apart and were each seven or eight feet from the interrupting task. In every case the alternative task or tasks and the main task were approximately the same distance from the interrupting task. This arrangement was substituted for that used in the preliminary experiment to avoid giving the alternative task an advantage over the main task by its position.

A second change in procedure was made in the conduct of the ex-

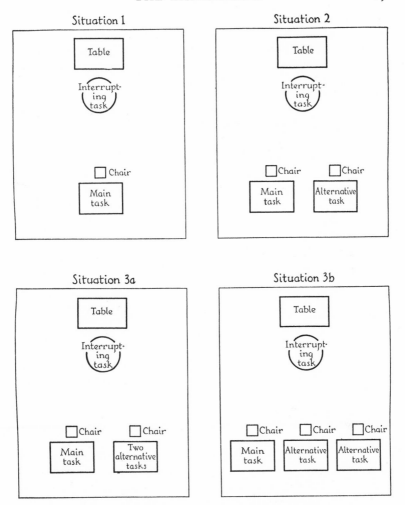

FIGURE 3.—PHYSICAL SETUP OF THE MAIN EXPERIMENT
In this arrangement the alternative and the main tasks were
approximately the same distance from the interrupting task.

periment after completion of the puzzle. In the preliminary work
it was found that most of the children did not wait for instructions
after finishing the puzzle but went immediately either to the interrupted task or to an alternative task. In the main experiment, therefore, after the child had finished the puzzle the experimenter ig-
nored him and wrote a description of his behavior, leaving him free

to engage in an activity or to leave the room. In a few cases the child watched the experimenter and appeared to be waiting for instructions. This behavior was common among unusually shy or inhibited children. If the child was still waiting after thirty seconds he was given the same instructions as were used in the preliminary investigation.

To facilitate the treatment of the results, the main investigation is regarded as consisting of four separate experiments, each of the first three including 108 single experiments. In Experiment A the interruption occurred near the beginning of the task, in Experiment B near the middle, and in Experiment C when the task was about three-fourths complete; in Experiment D there were 162 experiments with the interruption near the end of the task. Table 1 gives the exact point at which the interruption of the various tasks occurred in the four experiments.

TABLE I.—PERCENTAGE OF THE VARIOUS TASKS COMPLETED AT THE TIME
OF INTERRUPTION

Task	Percentage of Task Completed at Time of Interruption			
	Experiment A	Experiment B	Experiment C	Experiment D
Mosaic	15	52	74	85
Christmas tree . . .	15	54	73	85
Balloons	14	57	71	86
Easter basket. . . .	13	53	73	87
Sewing.	13	53	73	87
Matching game . . .	14	57	71	86

Each of the six tasks was used as the interrupted task an equal number of times in each of the three situations. In Experiments A, B, and C, respectively, each task was used as the interrupted task six times in each situation, in Experiment D nine times in each situation. This alternation of tasks was necessary since there was no reason to suppose that the tasks were equal in interest value. In the absence of such equality a serious error might be made if a task were used more frequently in one situation than in another. Let us suppose, for example, that the Christmas tree is the most interesting task and the crayoning of balloons the least interesting. If the tree were used most frequently in Situation I and the crayoning most frequently in Situation II, a lower percentage of resumption in Situation II than in Situation I might be due to the fact that the main task was the less interesting rather than to the presence of an alternative task.

In the preliminary investigation and in the first experiments of the main investigation the three situations were presented to the child on different days, usually on three successive days. Because of absences some of the children were available for only one or two experiments. In most of the experiments, however, the child was presented with all three situations on the same day, and short intermissions were allowed between the experiments. This latter method proved to be more economical in terms of the investigator's time and was not too long a period for the child. The three situations together usually required from 30 to 45 minutes.

IQ's were obtained for the subjects by means of the Goodenough Man-Drawing Test (3). This test was used because the time required for administration is relatively short, usually not over five minutes for children of kindergarten age. The test correlates .86 with the Stanford-Binet at four and one-half years and .70 at five and one-half years. It is admittedly a rough measure of intelligence, but it was not regarded as essential for this experiment to have an instrument that would make fine distinctions. It was intended only to serve the function of picking out the very bright and the dull children and of eliminating feeble-minded subjects from the group. The test was given following one of the experimental situations.

Two groups of subjects were not tested for intelligence—the children in a public school kindergarten and the children in the kindergarten of the Institute of Child Welfare of the University of Minnesota. Both these groups had received formal instruction in the drawing of the human figure. Such training would undoubtedly have affected the test results, and hence any IQ's obtained for these children could not have been regarded as even reasonably accurate measures of intelligence.

The writer's general impression is that, for the most part, the children thoroughly enjoyed the experiments. Typical questions were:

"Why did you choose me to play these games?"

"Why did you buy all these games for us to play with?"

"Are you going to let Robert play these games too?"

"Don't you have some more games?"

"Can I do the Christmas tree again?"

"Can I do the games again tomorrow?"

"Will you bring some more games tomorrow?"

III. QUANTITATIVE RESULTS

The behavior occurring after interruption of the main task may be classified into four main types:

1. Complete resumption: resumption and completion of the interrupted activity.

2. Failure to resume: failure to continue the interrupted activity. The subject leaves the room or engages in another activity but does not return to the main task.

3. Partial resumption: resumption but not completion of the interrupted activity.

4. Delayed resumption: resumption after the subject has completed or partially completed one or two alternative tasks.

In the statistical analysis, it has seemed desirable to make, in addition to this fourfold classification, a twofold classification of the behavior in which all the above types of behavior would be classified either as resumption or nonresumption. The question then arises as to how to classify cases of partial resumption and delayed resumption. In partial resumption the subject resumes the task immediately after the interruption but does not complete it, while in delayed resumption he completes the task but does not resume at the *earliest* opportunity after interruption. Theoretical considerations have led us to classify partial resumption as resumption and delayed resumption as nonresumption. The chief reason for regarding delayed resumption as a form of nonresumption is that it lacks the characteristic of immediacy. In discussing the nature of the tension system, Lewin states that a "tendency may readily be observed toward immediate discharge of tension" (4, page 59). Ovsiankina, also, emphasizes the factor of immediacy. If in her experiments the subject had not resumed the interrupted activity 15 to 20 seconds after finishing the interrupting task, she passed on to the next part of the experiment. In another situation the subject was left alone in the room for a time with completed tasks and tasks that he had failed to complete when he had been given an opportunity earlier in the experiment to do so. Some of the subjects resumed the uncompleted tasks under these conditions, but the author is careful to point out that such resumption is to be distinguished from the type which occurs immediately after the interruption and that it is probably due to a lack of any other available occupation.

A second argument against considering delayed resumption as resumption is based upon the results of the present investigation. In Situation II, of the subjects who resumed the main task immediately, 63 per cent completed the alternative task after finishing the original one. In Situation III, 59 per cent of the subjects who immediately resumed the main task completed both alternative tasks, and an additional 22 per cent completed one alternative task. Thus, well over half of the subjects did every task in the situation. This being the case, the subject who resumed the interrupted task after completing one or two alternative activities might have done so merely to be doing something. It would be incorrect, therefore, to classify such cases with those in which it is fairly clear that resumption is the result of a tension system set up by the incompleteness of the task.

Partial resumption, on the other hand, is qualitatively quite similar to complete resumption. It possesses the essential characteristic of immediacy—the subject returns to the interrupted activity at the earliest opportunity after interruption. In addition, an analysis of the three cases in which this type of behavior occurred left little doubt as to the existence in these individuals of a tension system corresponding to the interrupted task. In the first case, the subject set her own goal, which differed from the goal set by the experimenter. The task was the Easter basket, and she remarked, after pasting one row of paper eggs, "I won't put too many on—it will spoil it." Obviously she regarded the task as completed and did not consider it essential to use all the materials that the experimenter had provided.

In the second case, the subject remarked before the interruption that she did not crayon well. In spite of this, she resumed the crayoning task immediately after the interruption and made a few marks on one of the balloons. She then brought the paper to the experimenter and explained, "I don't like my crayoning. I only made one balloon." Perhaps the type of behavior involved can best be understood by referring to Lewin's concept of "valence." By the valence of an object is meant essentially its attraction for the individual. Lewin distinguishes "two large groups of valences according to the sort of initial behavior they elicit: the positive valences $(+)$, those effecting approach, and the negative $(-)$, or those producing withdrawal or retreat" (4, page 81). Furthermore, the same object may possess both a positive and a negative valence. For the subject under discussion the need or drive to complete the interrupted task may be regarded as a positive valence, dislike for the task as a negative valence. We can say, then, that the tension system corresponding to the positive valence was sufficiently strong after the interruption to gain temporary control of the motorium, but was too weak to keep this control in the face of a strong negative valence. But the chief point is that there did exist a tension system, corresponding to the positive valence, which was dominant long enough to lead to resumption on the part of the subject.

The behavior of the third subject was very similar to that of the one just considered. Before the interruption (which occurred after the coloring of one of the balloons) the subject expressed a desire to work at the "garden" (matching game) first and remarked that he didn't "color good." After the interruption he sat before the interrupted task, picked up a crayon and then put it down, with the comment, "Oh, gosh, I want to make the fruits first." The experimenter said nothing, and he immediately picked up the crayon again, remarking, "Oh, gosh, I don't want to color this—it's too hard for me." He crayoned three more balloons and gave the paper to the experimenter. "This is all I'll do today." He then completed the garden and left the room.

As in the preceding case, this behavior may be explained in terms of positive and negative valences. Again the need to complete the unfinished task may be looked upon as a positive valence, the subject's distaste for the activity as a negative valence. In addition, there is in this case a positive valence attached to the very attractive alternative task. In spite of these two seemingly strong valences acting to draw the subject away from the main task, the tension system corresponding to the positive valence of the main task was sufficiently effective to drive the subject to resume that task and to take possession of the motorium for a considerable period of time.

In the opinion of the writer, then, there is ample justification for including these three cases of partial resumption as cases of resumption, whereas delayed resumption cannot be regarded as true resumption in the sense that Lewin and his workers use the term. Consequently, in the presentation of the results, cases of complete resumption and partial resumption will be grouped together in calculating the total frequency of resumption; failure to resume and delayed resumption will be grouped together as nonresumption.

Effect of the point of interruption upon frequency of resump-

tion.—Table 2 summarizes the frequency of the four types of behavior in each of the three situations for the four points of interruption and the total frequency of each type of behavior for each point of interruption. It will be recalled that in Experiment A the interruption occurred near the beginning of the task; in B near the middle; in C when about three-fourths complete; in D at the end of the task.

TABLE 2.—FREQUENCY OF VARIOUS TYPES OF BEHAVIOR IN THE THREE SITUATIONS FOR DIFFERENT POINTS OF INTERRUPTION

Experiment and Situation	N^*	Type of Behavior											
		Complete Resumption		Partial Resumption		Delayed Resumption		Failure to Resume		Total Resumption		Total Nonresumption	
		N	%	N	%	N	%	N	%	N	%	N	%
A, total . .	108	97	90	3	3	4	4	4	4	100	93	8	7
A, I . . .	36	35	97	1	3	0	0	0	0	36	100	0	0
A, II . . .	36	32	89	1	3	2	6	1	3	33	92	3	8
A, III . .	36	30	83	1	3	2	6	3	8	31	86	5	14
B, total . .	108	98	91	0	0	2	2	8	7	98	91	10	9
B, I . . .	36	34	94	0	0	0	0	2	6	34	94	2	6
B, II . . .	36	33	92	0	0	1	3	2	6	33	92	3	8
B, III . .	36	31	86	0	0	1	3	4	11	31	86	5	14
C, total . .	108	100	93	0	0	0	0	8	7	100	93	8	7
C, I . . .	36	33	92	0	0	0	0	3	8	33	92	3	8
C, II . .	36	33	92	0	0	0	0	3	8	33	92	3	8
C, III . .	36	34	94	0	0	0	0	2	6	34	94	2	6
D, total . .	160	130	81	0	0	8	5	22	14	130	81	30	19
D, I . . .	53	46	87	0	0	0	0	7	13	46	87	7	13
D, II . .	54	42	78	0	0	3	6	9	17	42	78	12	22
D, III . .	53	42	79	0	0	5	9	6	11	42	79	11	21

* In Experiment D, although 162 situations were presented, there were only 160 interruptions, since one subject in Situation I and one in Situation III refused to be interrupted at all.

Table 3 gives the percentages of various types of behavior for the different points of interruption (A, B, C, and D); Table 4 computes the differences in these percentages as between each point of interruption and every other point of interruption. An inspection of these tables shows that there is only a slight difference in the frequency of occurrence of the various types of behavior in Experiments A, B, and C, or for interruption at the beginning,

Behavior	Experiments			
	A (N=108)	B (N=108)	C (N=108)	D (N=160)
Complete resumption	90	91	93	81
Partial resumption	3	0	0	0
Delayed resumption	4	2	0	5
Failure to resume	4	7	7	14
Total resumption	93	91	93	81
Total nonresumption . . .	7	9	7	19

middle, or three-fourths point of the task. There is no difference in the percentage of total resumption between Experiments A and C, and the critical ratios for the differences between A and B and between B and C are so small as to indicate that the slight differences that do appear are unreliable. The largest difference found in these three experiments is that between the percentage of delayed resumption in Experiments A and C. The difference of 4 per cent is 2.11 times the σ difference, indicating that there are 980 chances in 1,000 that there is a true difference between the two experiments in the frequency of this type of behavior.

Resumption is found to be less frequent when the interruption occurs near the end of the task than when it occurs earlier. The difference of 12 per cent in frequency of total resumption between Experiments A and D is 3.02 times the σ difference, which means that there are 999 chances in 1,000 that a true difference exists. The same critical ratio is found for the difference in total resumption between Experiments C and D. The critical ratio for Experiments B and D is slightly less (2.39), indicating that there are 992 chances in 1,000 of a true difference existing in the frequency of resumption as between these two points of interruption.

We may conclude, then, that under the conditions of this experiment and for subjects similar to the ones employed in it, an interrupted activity is resumed more frequently when the interruption occurs near the beginning of the task or when the subject has completed about three-fourths of the task than when it occurs near the end. There is also a distinct tendency for resumption to be more frequent with an interruption at about the middle of the task than with one near the end.

Since the percentage of complete resumption is the same as

TABLE 4.—DIFFERENCES IN PERCENTAGES BETWEEN THE VARIOUS TYPES OF BEHAVIOR IN EACH OF THE SEVERAL PAIRS OF EXPERIMENTS

Behavior	Diff.	σ Diff.*	$\dfrac{\text{Diff.}}{\sigma\,\text{Diff.}}$
EXPERIMENTS A AND B			
Complete resumption. . . .	− 1	4.03	− .25
Partial resumption	3	1.60	1.88
Delayed resumption	2	2.32	.86
Failure to resume	− 3	3.14	− .96
Total resumption.	2	3.75	.53
Total nonresumption . . .	− 2	3.75	− .53
EXPERIMENTS A AND C			
Complete resumption. . . .	− 3	3.83	− .78
Partial resumption	3	1.60	1.88
Delayed resumption	4	1.90	2.11
Failure to resume	− 3	3.14	− .96
Total resumption.	0		
Total nonresumption . . .	0		
EXPERIMENTS A AND D			
Complete resumption. . . .	9	4.25	2.12
Partial resumption	3	1.60	1.88
Delayed resumption	− 1	2.55	− .39
Failure to resume	−10	3.30	−3.03
Total resumption.	12	3.98	3.02
Total nonresumption . . .	−12	3.98	−3.02
EXPERIMENTS B AND C			
Complete resumption. . . .	− 2	3.75	− .53
Partial resumption	0		
Delayed resumption	2	1.30	1.54
Failure to resume	0		
Total resumption.	− 2	3.75	− .53
Total nonresumption . . .	2	3.75	.53
EXPERIMENTS B AND D			
Complete resumption. . . .	10	4.18	2.39
Partial resumption	0		
Delayed resumption	− 3	2.14	−1.40
Failure to resume	− 7	3.68	−1.90
Total resumption.	10	4.18	2.39
Total nonresumption . . .	−10	4.18	−2.39
EXPERIMENTS C AND D			
Complete resumption. . . .	12	3.98	3.02
Partial resumption	0		
Delayed resumption	− 5	1.70	−2.94
Failure to resume	− 7	3.68	−1.90
Total resumption.	12	3.98	3.02
Total nonresumption . . .	−12	3.98	−3.02

* The formula used in calculating the σ diff. was σ diff. $=\sqrt{\sigma_1{}^2+\sigma_2{}^2}$. Values for $\sigma_1{}^2$ were taken from the Table of Standard Errors and Probable Errors of Percentages for Varying Numbers of Cases, by Harold A. Edgerton and Donald G. Paterson, published in the *Journal of Applied Psychology*, 10: 378–91 (1926).

the percentage of total resumption for all the experiments except A, it is not surprising to find that the critical ratios indicate a tendency for this type of behavior, too, to occur more frequently in Experiments A, B, and C than in D. Two other differences are also of sufficient magnitude to warrant attention. The difference of 10 per cent between Experiments A and D in the behavior designated "failure to resume" is 3.03 times its standard error; and the difference of 5 per cent between Experiments C and D in the percentage of delayed resumption has a critical ratio of 2.94. Thus we may conclude that, if the interruption comes at the end of the task, a larger percentage of the subjects will fail to resume than if it occurs at the beginning, and a larger percentage will exhibit delayed resumption than if it occurs at a point where the task is about three-fourths complete.

TABLE 5.—COMPARISON OF OVSIANKINA'S AND KATZ'S PERCENTAGES OF RESUMPTION
FOR VARIOUS POINTS OF INTERRUPTION

Point of Interruption	Ovsiankina		Katz		Diff.	σ Diff.	Diff. σ Diff.
	No.	Per Cent	No.	Per Cent			
Beginning . . .	32	92	108	93	− 1	5.42	− .18
Middle.	142	84	108	91	− 7	4.18	−1.67
Three-fourths. .	45	72	108	93	−21	6.99	−3.00
End	97	83	160	81	2	4.91	.40

In Table 5 the results of the present study are compared with Ovsiankina's (9) main findings on the effect of the point of interruption on frequency of resumption. It is clear that the most significant difference between the two experiments in the frequency of resumption is at the point designated by Ovsiankina as the middle-end, which is the same as our point of three-fourths completion. The critical ratio of 3.0 indicates that there are 999 chances out of 1,000 that there is a true difference between the two experiments in the frequency of resumption at this point. Furthermore, in Ovsiankina's experiment, the difference of 20 per cent between resumption when the interruption was at the beginning and when it was at the middle-end is 2.43 times the σ difference, which points to a tendency for resumption to be greater at the beginning than at the middle-end. No such trend is present in our data. These differences between the two experiments may be accounted for in various ways. There was a marked difference in the tasks, in the choice of subjects, and in the physical setup of the two experiments. Any one or all of these factors may have contributed to produce the different results. In the opinion of the author, Ovsiankina is not warranted in concluding from her data that the tension system decreases gradually from the beginning of the task to the point where it is about three-fourths complete and then increases again just before the goal is reached. The difference of 8 per cent between the beginning and middle points is 1.40 times its standard error, the difference of 12 per cent between the middle and middle-end 1.63 times its standard error, and the difference of 11 per cent between the middle-end and end 1.43 times its standard error. None of these critical ratios is sufficiently high to establish definitely the presence of differences between the frequency of interruption at successive points of interruption. It is certainly unjustifiable to speak of a sudden rise in tension at the end of the task, for the difference of 11 per cent between the percentage who resumed with interruption at the middle-end and the percentage who resumed with interruption near the end is only 1.43 times its standard error. In addition, the small number of cases in which the interruption occurred at the beginning or middle-end demands that caution be used in drawing conclusions on the basis of these data.

Turning now to the interpretation of the results of the present investigation, we find it necessary to inquire what these data mean in terms of the tension system set up within the individual. As we have pointed out, Ovsiankina interprets her results to mean that tension decreases as the task progresses until it is about three-fourths complete and then increases. Such an interpretation appears to the writer to be quite contrary to Lewin's fundamental viewpoint. In his book Lewin (4) points out fallacies in the psychologist's "attempts at quantitative determination." He considers, for example, the experimental work that has been done to determine the strength of various drives in rats. "The various possible degrees of strength of the several drives are ascertained and their maximal strengths are compared. It is true, of course, that the Aristotelian attitude is really only slightly ameliorated thereby. The curve expresses the statistical average of a large number of cases, which is not binding for an individual case" (4, page 38).

Similarly in Ovsiankina's work and in the present investigation the percentages give only the frequency of resumption for a whole group and tell us nothing about the tension system in the individual case. It is entirely possible that a high frequency of resumption for a group may not be associated with a strong tension system in the individuals of that group and that a low frequency does not necessarily denote a weak tension system in the individual subjects. Figure 4 may help to clarify this point. The horizontal lines designate the threshold for resumption; i. e., the tension system in the individual must be sufficiently strong to rise above this threshold

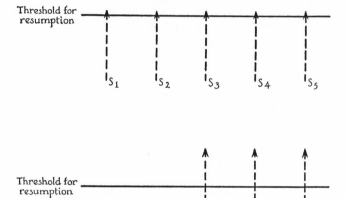

FIGURE 4.—HYPOTHETICAL ILLUSTRATION OF THE THRESHOLD
FOR RESUMPTION

The tension system must arise above the threshold if resumption is to occur. In the first case, in which the interruption occurred at the beginning of the task, resumption was 100 per cent complete, though weak in every instance. In the second case, in which interruption occurred near the end, there was only 60 per cent resumption, though the tension was very strong in these three cases.

if resumption is to occur. The vertical arrows designate the strength of the tension system for different subjects. Let us suppose, for the purpose of clarification, that the upper part of Figure 4 represents the state of tension in five subjects who have been interrupted at the beginning of a task and the lower part the tension of five subjects who have been interrupted at the end of a task. The tension system in the subjects interrupted at the beginning is just barely strong enough in each case to pass the threshold and thus there is a 100 per cent resumption. On the other hand, only 60 per cent of the subjects interrupted at the end of the task resume. In Subjects 1 and

2 the tension system is too weak to pass the threshold, while in Subjects 3, 4, and 5 the tension system is very strong—much stronger than for any of the subjects interrupted at the beginning. There is no reason to suppose that these hypothetical situations could not or do not exist. It is clear, then, that although a larger proportion of a total group of subjects may resume under one set of conditions than under another, it cannot be inferred from this that the tension system is stronger in the subjects of the first group than in those of the second.

Consequently, the only conclusion that may safely be drawn from the data on the point of interruption is that, under the conditions of this experiment, when the task is interrupted near the end, a tension system sufficiently strong to drive the subject to resume is set up in fewer cases than when the task is interrupted near the beginning, middle, or at a point where it is approximately three-fourths complete.

Effect of alternative activities upon frequency of resumption.— The next problem to be considered is whether the presence in the experimental situation of tasks other than the interrupted one reduces the frequency of resumption. The hypothesis proposed in the introduction was that if the subject was given the opportunity to engage in another activity after the interruption, he might be as likely to take up the new activity as to finish the interrupted one.

At this point brief mention must be made again of the fact that in Experiments B and D the physical setup of Situation III was not the same for all the subjects. In 49 of the experiments the two alternative tasks were on the same table and in 41 on two different tables. In order to determine whether this variation in procedure affected the results, a comparison was made of the frequency of resumption under the two sets of conditions. Forty-nine subjects for whom the alternative tasks were placed on one table resumed in 81 per cent of the experiments, whereas 41 subjects for whom the alternative tasks were placed on two tables resumed in 85 per cent of the experiments. The small difference of 4 per cent is only .51 times the σ difference, indicating that there is not a significant difference between the two setups and that, therefore, they may be analyzed together.

Table 6 gives the frequency with which the various types of behavior occurred in the three situations. In Situation I, where only the interrupted task was present, resumption occurred in 93 per cent of the cases; in Situation II, where the interrupted task and one other were present, resumption occurred in 87 per cent of the cases; and in Situation III, where the interrupted task and two others were present, resumption occurred in 86 per cent of the cases. The difference of 1 per cent between Situations II and III is small and statistically insignificant. The difference of 6 per cent between Situations I and II is 1.83 times its standard error and the difference of 7 per cent between Situations I and III is 2.08 times

TABLE 6.—FREQUENCY OF THE VARIOUS TYPES OF BEHAVIOR IN
THE THREE SITUATIONS*

($N = 162$ in each situation)

Behavior	Situation I		Situation II		Situation III		Total	
	No.	Per Cent	No.	Per Cent	No.	Per Cent	No.	Per Cent
Complete resumption . . .	148	92	140	86	137	85	425	88
Partial resumption	1	1	1	1	1	1	3	1
Delayed resumption	0	0	6	4	8	5	14	3
Failure to resume	12	7	15	9	15	9	42	9
Total resumption	149	93	141	87	138	86	428	88
Total nonresumption . .	12	7	21	13	23	14	56	12

* Two subjects refused to be interrupted, one in Situation I, one in Situation III.

its standard error. There are, therefore, about 960 chances in 1,000 of a true difference between Situations I and II and about 980 chances in 1,000 of a true difference between Situations I and III in the frequency of resumption. Thus, there is some indication of a tendency for the percentage of resumption to decrease slightly with the addition of tasks other than the interrupted one, though the results are not conclusive. In any event, the differences found are exceedingly small in absolute magnitude.

One conclusion, however, may unquestionably be drawn from the results of this phase of the investigation. The statement was made in Chapter I that in previous investigations it could not be definitely ascertained whether resumption occurred because of a specific tension system corresponding to the interrupted task or merely because of a need of the individual for activity of some sort. The results of our experiments with Situations II and III provide a clear answer to that question. Let us assume that the subject is driven merely by the need for activity. Then, in Situation II, he would be as likely to choose the alternative task as the main task, other things being equal. Under such conditions, resumption would occur in about 50 per cent of the cases. If the same assumption is made with regard to Situation III, where there are two alternative tasks and the interrupted task, resumption might be expected to occur in about 33⅓ per cent of the cases. (We might even expect resumption to occur in a still smaller percentage of cases, since the subject was always free to leave the situation if he chose.) However, 87 per cent resumed in Situation II—37 per cent more than the expected frequency; and 86 per cent resumed in Situation III—53 per cent more than the expected frequency. Such results furnish unequivocal evidence that an interrupted task has an advantage over a task on which the subject has not worked. It is quite possible, of course, that in some cases the interrupted task was more interesting to the subject than the alternative task or tasks, but in view of the fact that each task was used as the main task and alternative task an equal number of times, this could not have happened in enough instances to account for the high percentage of resumption in Situations II and III. In order to obtain such results for the group as a whole, it would be necessary to assume that, by chance, a main task was chosen for the majority of subjects which was more interesting to them than the alternative task or tasks. Since this is a very remote possibility, the only possible explanation of the phenomenon is that it was the incompleteness of the task that led to resumption.

These data, then, definitely support the findings of Lewin and his workers. In fact, in this investigation resumption occurred in an even larger proportion of cases than other investigators report. Ovsiankina (9) and Lissner (6) found resumption percentages of 83 and 85 respectively when the interruption was accomplished by giving the subject another task to perform; the present author obtained resumption after 88 per cent of the 484 interruptions. The outstanding fact is that substantially the same results were obtained in this investigation as in the other two, in spite of the great difference in the character of the subjects, in the tasks, and in the experimental setups.

Effect of alternative activities upon frequency of resumption for different points of interruption.—In view of the fact that resumption was found to be less frequent when the interruption occurred near the end of the task than when it occurred earlier, it is necessary to consider the third question formulated in the introduction. Does the effect of the presence of an alternative activity upon resumption of the main activity depend in any way upon the stage of the task at which interruption occurs? It is entirely possible that the presence of alternative tasks in the situation might have the greatest effect upon resumption when, in general, resumption is least likely to occur. That is, we might expect that the differences between Situations I and II and I and III would be greater when the interruption occurs near the end of the activity than when it occurs at one of the other points. An inspection of Table 7, however, fails to confirm this hypothesis.

TABLE 7.—COMPARISON OF THE TOTAL PERCENTAGES OF RESUMPTION IN THE THREE TEST SITUATIONS

Experiment	Percentages of Resumption		Diff.	σ Diff.	Diff. / σ Diff.
	Situation I	Situation II			
A	100 (N= 36)	92 (N= 36)	8	4.50	1.78
B	94 (N= 36)	92 (N= 36)	2	6.02	.33
C	92 (N= 36)	92 (N= 36)	0		
D	87 (N= 53)	78 (N= 54)	9	7.25	1.24
Total. . .	93 (N=161)	87 (N=162)	6	3.28	1.83
	Situation I	Situation III			
A	100 (N= 36)	86 (N= 36)	14	5.80	2.41
B	94 (N= 36)	86 (N= 36)	8	7.05	1.13
C	92 (N= 36)	94 (N= 36)	−2	6.02	−.33
D	87 (N= 53)	79 (N= 53)	8	7.25	1.10
Total. . .	93 (N=161)	86 (N=161)	7	3.36	2.08
	Situation II	Situation III			
A	92 (N= 36)	86 (N= 36)	6	7.34	.82
B	92 (N= 36)	86 (N= 36)	6	7.34	.82
C	92 (N= 36)	94 (N= 36)	−2	6.02	−.33
D	78 (N= 54)	79 (N= 53)	−1	7.92	−.13
Total. . .	87 (N=162)	86 (N=161)	1	3.75	.27

The difference between Situations I and II is less significant in Experiment D (where the lowest percentage of resumption occurred) than in Experiment A (where the highest percentage of resumption occurred), and less significant in Experiment D than in all the experiments combined. A similar tendency is found for the difference between Situations I and III. Although the number of cases for each situation at each point of interruption is too few to warrant a broad generalization, there is obviously no reason to suppose, on the basis of these data, that alternative tasks have a differential effect upon resumption at different points of interruption.

Effect of the nature of the main task upon frequency of resumption.—Table 8 gives the frequency of various types of behavior for each task employed as the main or interrupted activity. It is clear that resumption does not occur with equal frequency for all

TABLE 8.—FREQUENCY OF VARIOUS TYPES OF BEHAVIOR FOR EACH TASK EMPLOYED AS THE MAIN TASK

Behavior	Mosaic		Tree		Basket		Sewing		Matching		Balloons	
	No.	%	No.	%	No.	%	No.	%	No.	%	No.	%
Complete resumption. .	79	98	76	95	72	89	68	84	66	83	64	79
Partial resumption . . .	0	0	0	0	1	1	0	0	0	0	2	2
Delayed resumption . .	2	2	0	0	2	2	3	4	5	6	2	2
Failure to resume . . .	0	0	4	5	6	7	10	12	9	11	13	16
Total resumption . .	79	98	76	95	73	90	68	84	66	83	66	81
Total nonresumption .	2	2	4	5	8	10	13	16	14	17	15	19

the tasks. The number of interruptions in the mosaic, basket, sewing, and balloon tasks were 81 in each case; the number of interruptions in the tree and matching tasks were 80 in each case.

In Table 9 each task is compared with every other task in regard to the frequency of occurrence of the various types of behavior. The greatest difference occurs between the mosaic and balloon tasks, the mosaic being resumed in 98 per cent of the cases and the balloons in only 81 per cent. The difference of 17 per cent is 3.63 times the σ difference, indicating that there are 999 chances in 1,000 that a true difference exists between these tasks. The other results may be summarized briefly:

1. There is almost certainly a true difference in the frequency of resumption between the mosaic and matching (critical ratio of 3.33) and mosaic and sewing (critical ratio of 3.18). This difference is in favor of the mosaic.

2. There is a tendency for resumption to occur more frequently for the mosaic than for the basket (critical ratio of 2.18); for the tree than for the sewing (critical ratio of 2.32); for the tree than for the matching (critical ratio of 2.48); for the tree than for the balloons (critical ratio of 2.79).

3. The remaining critical ratios are too small to indicate differences between the tasks.

The differences noted may have been due to differences in the interest value of the various tasks. It is entirely possible that the crayoning of balloons had the least appeal, since the task involved

Behavior	Tasks Compared		Diff.	σ Diff.	Diff. / σ Diff.
	Mosaic	Tree			
Complete resumption.	98	95	3	2.89	1.04
Partial resumption	0	0	0		
Delayed resumption	2	0	2	1.60	1.25
Failure to resume	0	5	− 5	2.40	−2.08
Total resumption.	98	95	3	2.89	1.04
Total nonresumption	2	5	− 3	2.89	−1.04
	Mosaic	Basket			
Complete resumption.	98	89	9	3.85	2.34
Partial resumption	0	1	− 1	1.10	− .91
Delayed resumption	2	2	0		
Failure to resume	0	7	− 7	2.80	−2.50
Total resumption.	98	90	8	3.67	2.18
Total nonresumption	2	10	− 8	3.67	−2.18
	Mosaic	Sewing			
Complete resumption.	98	84	14	4.40	3.18
Partial resumption	0	0	0		
Delayed resumption	2	4	− 2	2.72	− .74
Failure to resume	0	12	−12	3.60	−3.33
Total resumption.	98	84	14	4.40	3.18
Total nonresumption	2	16	−14	4.40	−3.18
	Mosaic	Matching			
Complete resumption.	98	83	15	4.50	3.33
Partial resumption	0	0	0		
Delayed resumption	2	6	− 4	3.14	−1.27
Failure to resume	0	11	−11	3.50	−3.14
Total resumption.	98	83	15	4.50	3.33
Total nonresumption	2	17	−15	4.50	−3.33
	Mosaic	Balloons			
Complete resumption.	98	79	19	4.78	3.97
Partial resumption	0	2	− 2	1.60	−1.25
Delayed resumption	2	2	0		
Failure to resume	0	16	−16	4.10	−3.90
Total resumption.	98	81	17	4.68	3.63
Total nonresumption	2	19	−17	4.68	−3.63
	Tree	Basket			
Complete resumption.	95	89	6	4.24	1.42
Partial resumption	0	1	− 1	1.10	− .91
Delayed resumption	0	2	− 2	1.60	−1.25
Failure to resume	5	7	− 2	3.69	− .54
Total resumption.	95	90	5	4.08	1.23
Total nonresumption	5	10	− 5	4.08	−1.23
	Tree	Sewing			
Complete resumption.	95	84	11	4.75	2.32
Partial resumption	0	0	0		
Delayed resumption	0	4	− 4	2.20	−1.82
Failure to resume	5	12	− 7	4.33	−1.62
Total resumption.	95	84	11	4.75	2.32
Total nonresumption	5	16	−11	4.75	−2.32

TABLE 9.—*Continued*

Behavior	Tasks Compared		Diff.	σ Diff.	Diff. / σ Diff.
	Tree	Matching			
Complete resumption.	95	83	12	4.84	2.48
Partial resumption	0	0	0		
Delayed resumption	0	6	− 6	2.70	−2.22
Failure to resume	5	11	− 6	4.24	−1.42
Total resumption.	95	83	12	4.84	2.48
Total nonresumption	5	17	−12	4.84	−2.48
	Tree	Balloons			
Complete resumption.	95	79	16	5.09	3.14
Partial resumption	0	2	− 2	1.60	−1.25
Delayed resumption	0	2	− 2	1.60	−1.25
Failure to resume	5	16	−11	4.75	−2.32
Total resumption.	95	81	14	5.01	2.79
Total nonresumption	5	19	−14	5.01	−2.79
	Basket	Sewing			
Complete resumption.	89	84	5	5.39	.93
Partial resumption	1	0	1	1.10	.91
Delayed resumption	2	4	− 2	2.72	− .74
Failure to resume	7	12	− 5	4.56	−1.10
Total resumption.	90	84	6	5.26	1.14
Total nonresumption	10	16	− 6	5.26	−1.14
	Basket	Matching			
Complete resumption.	89	83	6	5.47	1.10
Partial resumption	1	0	1	1.10	.91
Delayed resumption	2	6	− 4	3.14	−1.27
Failure to resume	7	11	− 4	4.48	− .89
Total resumption.	90	83	7	5.34	1.31
Total nonresumption	10	17	− 7	5.34	−1.31
	Basket	Balloons			
Complete resumption.	89	79	10	5.70	1.75
Partial resumption	1	2	− 1	1.94	− .52
Delayed resumption	2	2	0		
Failure to resume	7	16	− 9	4.97	−1.81
Total resumption.	90	81	9	5.50	1.64
Total nonresumption	10	19	− 9	5.50	−1.64
	Sewing	Matching			
Complete resumption.	84	83	1	5.87	.17
Partial resumption	0	0	0		
Delayed resumption	4	6	− 2	3.48	− .57
Failure to resume	12	11	1	5.02	.20
Total resumption.	84	83	1	5.87	.17
Total nonresumption	16	17	− 1	5.87	− .17
	Sewing	Balloons			
Complete resumption.	84	79	5	6.09	.82
Partial resumption	0	2	− 2	1.60	−1.25
Delayed resumption	4	2	2	2.72	.74
Failure to resume	12	16	− 4	5.46	− .73
Total resumption.	84	81	3	6.02	.50
Total nonresumption	16	19	− 3	6.02	− .50

TABLE 9.—*Continued*

Behavior	Tasks Compared		Diff.	σ Diff.	Diff. / σ Diff.
	Matching	Balloons			
Complete resumption.	83	79	4	6.16	.65
Partial resumption	0	2	− 2	1.60	−1.25
Delayed resumption	6	2	4	3.14	1.27
Failure to resume	11	16	− 5	5.39	− .93
Total resumption.	83	81	2	6.08	.33
Total nonresumption	17	19	− 2	6.08	− .33

a type of activity very familiar to the nursery school and kindergarten child. The mosaic, on the other hand, probably held the child's interest because of its novelty. The tree also had the advantage of being an unfamiliar activity.

Another factor that may account for the fact that the greatest difference between any two tasks was that between the mosaic and the balloons is the relative difficulty of the two tasks. Ovsiankina (9) found that such tasks as making plasticine figures or solving puzzles were resumed more frequently than tasks like cross-hatching or unwinding a ball of thread. She regards this tendency as being partly due to the fact that the problem nature of the former activities results in a strong goal-tension being aroused in the subject. This finding is interesting in view of the fact that the mosaic was certainly the most difficult of the six tasks used in the present investigation. The majority of the subjects asked the experimenter for aid with it at some point, and those who did not definitely request help usually inquired whether they were putting in the blocks correctly. The balloons, on the other hand, presented no problem, since all the subjects knew how to crayon. It is more difficult to account for the differences between the tree and the other tasks. The tree task was undoubtedly of great interest to the subjects because of its novelty, but it was not difficult. Probably the interest factor alone was sufficient to account for the high frequency of resumption.

The significant finding of the analysis of the tasks, however, is that resumption does vary with the nature of the main activity, which means that in investigations of this problem it is essential to give some attention to the type of task chosen for the interrupted activity.

Relationship between frequency of resumption and intelligence. — In order to determine whether there was any relationship between the tendency to resume interrupted activities and intelligence (within the range of normal intelligence), two groups of subjects were compared. The first group consisted of subjects whose IQ's were between 79 and 100 on the Goodenough Man-Drawing Test. The second group was made up of subjects with IQ's from 120 to 153. Because the test gives only a rough measure of intelligence, these two widely separated groups were chosen. The investigator was thus practically assured of two groups that really differed in intelligence. Rarely would a subject included in the lower group have a true IQ sufficiently high to be classified in the superior group (i. e., 20 points or more higher than the obtained IQ). And just as infrequently would a subject in the superior group have a true IQ of 100 or less.

The children in the inferior IQ group were subjects in 117 experiments and resumed in 85 per cent of them. The superior group were subjects in 91 experiments and resumed in 90 per cent of them. The critical ratio of the difference is 1.10, which is too small to indicate any real difference between the two groups in frequency of resumption. Thus, within the range of IQ's considered in this study, intelligence was not a factor determining the frequency of resumption.

Relationship between frequency of resumption and socio-economic status.—The necessity of obtaining a large number of subjects within a very limited age range made it virtually impossible, from a practical standpoint, to select a group of subjects that could be considered representative, in socio-economic status, of the population at large. It was also impossible to equate the groups used in the four main experiments on the basis of socio-economic status. It is therefore of some importance to know to what extent this type of heterogeneity affected the results.

The method used to determine this effect was to compare two groups of children from widely separated socio-economic classes. One group was made up of children from kindergartens and nursery schools in settlement houses, who, without exception, came from underprivileged homes. The other group included children from the nursery school and kindergarten of the Institute of Child Welfare of the University of Minnesota, children from a public school kindergarten in a well-to-do suburb of Cleveland, Ohio, and a small number of subjects from a private nursery school in Cleveland. The children in this second group came from homes distinctly above the average in socio-economic status.

It was found that the children in the higher group resumed in 89 per cent of the 96 experiments, and the children in the lower group resumed in 86 per cent of the 208 experiments. There is a small difference of 3 per cent in favor of the higher socio-economic group, but this is only .75 times the σ difference. The obvious conclusion to be drawn is that, for this sampling of subjects, socio-economic status cannot be considered a factor influencing resumption.

IV. QUALITATIVE RESULTS

In the preceding chapter the responses of the subjects were classified into categories which took account only of relatively broad aspects of behavior. This was essential for a quantitative treatment of the data. In the present chapter an attempt will be made to deal with qualitatively different types of behavior within these broad categories and to get a clearer picture of the behavior of individual subjects. To accomplish this, it is necessary to consider not only behavior which occurs repeatedly but also that which is shown by only one or two subjects.

Table 10 presents a detailed analysis of the various types of behavior manifested by the subjects who resumed the interrupted activity. Many of the responses listed in the table may be regarded as indicative of the existence of a tension system or need to complete the interrupted task. This is true, for example, of the type of behavior designated in the table as "resistance to interruption." Ovsiankina (9) likewise found that interruption was often accompanied by protests and irritation on the part of the subject, and in some cases by a continuation of the task in spite of the experimenter's demand that the subject do something else. Several instances of the three types of resistance to interruption mentioned in the table follow:

1. Verbal resistance:
   Main task, the basket. When experimenter (E) interrupted, subject (S) replied, "As soon as I finish these."
   Main task, the tree. S's response to the interruption was: "I want to finish this first."

2. Continuation with the task:
   Main task, the matching. S put in one more disc before E could stop her.
   Main task, the basket. S pasted another egg before obeying E's command to work on the puzzle.

3. Verbal resistance and continuation with the task:
   Main task, the mosaic. S added two more blocks after E had interrupted. "I'll finish this first." He resumed immediately after the interruption. "Now what shall I do? I'll finish my man."

41

TABLE 10.—FREQUENCY OF VARIOUS TYPES OF BEHAVIOR IN CASES OF RESUMPTION

Type of Behavior	Frequency of Occurrence			
	Situation I	Situation II	Situation III	Total
Conditions of resumption:				
Resumes immediately after interruption . . .	128	105	98	331
Runs to resume.	5	7	4	16
Delays few seconds before resuming (talks to experimenter, etc.)	6	7	7	20
Resumes after directions given	7	9	5	21
Asks experimenter's permission to resume . .	1		3	4
Resumes before finishing puzzle.	1	1		2
Resumes but does not complete task.	1	1	1	3
Resumes after approaching alternative task by mistake		7	4	11
Looks at alternative task or tasks as he resumes		3	1	4
Looks at, talks about, or handles alternative task before resuming.			4	4
Wavers between alternative and main task, but resumes main task.			1	1
Resistance to interruption:				
Continues with task	3	2	3	8
Resists verbally.	3	6	4	13
Completes task	1		1	2
Behavior after interruption:				
Expresses intention to continue or finish main task, or feeling that main task must be finished, or satisfaction at being allowed to return	20	22	23	65
Remarks about incompleteness of task, amount still to be done, etc.	11	6	6	23
Impatience shown during interruption		1	1	2
Marked interest shown in alternative task:				
Asks to do alternative task first.		5	1	6
Asks questions about alternative task while doing main task.		1		1
Expresses intention of doing alternative task while completing main task or while doing puzzle		2	1	3
Behavior with respect to alternative task:				
Does alternative task immediately after main task		89	30	119
Does alternative task after permission granted		6	1	7
Does both alternative tasks after main task . .			82	82
Completes one alternative task and partially completes another.			3	3
Partially completes one alternative task . . .			1	1
Starts alternative tasks but does not finish them			1	1
Asks to do alternative task after one of other experiments		1	1	2
Does not do alternative task or tasks		45	19	64

Various remarks made by the subject after the interruption may also be considered evidence of the existence of a strong drive to finish the uncompleted task:

1. Remarks concerning the incompleteness of the task or the amount still to be done:
   "Just one more."
   "I might as well work on this. I'm not through with it yet."
   "I haven't done all this yet."
   "Some more things to put in."
   "I have just these two to do yet."
   "The balloons aren't all colored yet." (This subject started toward the interrupted task and then hesitated and looked at E. As soon as the directions were given he hurried to finish the interrupted task.)

2. A desire expressed to complete the interrupted task:
   "Have you any more puzzles? But maybe I better finish these."
   "Now I have to finish this. Only two more."
   "Me finish."
   "Shall I go to finish my man picture?" (as he ran back to the mosaic).
   "Me almost done."

3. The task spoken of as a "job":
   "Now can I do my own job?"
   "I'm going to do my own job that I was doing."
   "I'll have to do my business now."

4. Intention or need expressed to continue with interrupted task:
   "I need to do this again."
   "I'll do my basket some more, I guess."
   "I'll go back and do this."
   "Now I can go back to the other thing."

A still further and quite significant indication of the existence of a need to complete the interrupted main activity is provided by the behavior of many of the subjects with reference to the alternative task or tasks in Situations II and III.

1. Immediate resumption of the main task after interruption in spite of an expressed desire before the interruption to work at the alternative task:
   S asked to work at the tree instead of the sewing. Commented on sewing, "This is hard." Ran back to main task after the interruption. Then completed the tree.

S asked to work at the tree instead of the balloons. Resisted interruption. "I'll do that puzzle as soon as I finish this." Resumed immediately, then completed the tree.

At the beginning S asked to do the sewing instead of the balloons, but did not do the sewing until he had completed the balloons.

2. Looking at or handling the alternative task or tasks before resuming the main task:

S handled the alternative tasks. "Look at all the lights." S resumed the main task, then completed both alternative tasks.

S picked up one of the alternative tasks. "Can you make this with any color you want?" (referring to sewing). S then resumed the main task, then completed both alternative tasks.

At the beginning S said he wanted to work at one of the alternative tasks (tree) instead of the main task. After interruption looked at alternative tasks but resumed main task.

S sat before the alternative task. "Can you take the man out?" E said "No." "What can I do now?" E answered that he could do anything he wished. He resumed the main task immediately, then did the alternative tasks.

S looked at the alternative tasks but resumed. "I'll finish this first." Then she did the alternative tasks.

3. Approaching the alternative task after the interruption but immediately turning back to the main task:

S walked up to the table on which the alternative task was placed, but immediately resumed the main task. "I forgot what table I was at."

S discovered his mistake just as he was about to sit down before the alternative task. "Oh, I thought I was sitting here."

S ran to the table on which the alternative task was placed. When he saw it he turned and ran immediately to the main task.

S sat down before the alternative task but immediately got up and resumed the main task.

S walked to the table on which the alternative tasks were placed but immediately turned away and ran to the main task. "I have to finish this first."

4. An intention expressed to work at the alternative task after completing the main task:

"After I get this done, I can do the Christmas tree one."

"Now can I finish this one? *Then* I'll do the other one. I like these games."

In the following cases, the subjects complained about the main task but nevertheless completed it, a fact that supports Ovsiankina's (9) observation that even uninteresting tasks are often resumed.

1. "I don't like this game" (sewing). After the interruption S resumed immediately and completed the task.
2. After the interruption S remarked, "I'm getting tired of doing this." Nevertheless he completed the task.
3. S complained before the interruption that his hand was tired from pressing on the crayon and rested it for a short time. After the interruption he resumed immediately.

TABLE 11.—FREQUENCY OF VARIOUS TYPES OF BEHAVIOR IN CASES OF NONRESUMPTION

Type of Behavior	Frequency of Occurrence			
	Situation I	Situation II	Situation III	Total
Resistance to interruption:				
Continues with task	1	1		2
Verbal resistance		1		1
Asks for another game or asks to write	1	1	3	5
Looks at main task before leaving room		1		1
Looks at main task as he leaves room	1	1		2
Leaves room after directions	6	2	1	9
Leaves room before directions	1		2	3
Talks or handles tasks, then leaves room	1	2		3
After interruption brings task to experimenter	2			2
Asks to do task he did not do in another experiment	1			1
Asks to do one of tasks of another experiment again or to draw another man	2			2
Does alternative task after interruption, does not resume		9	2	11
Does both alternative tasks, does not resume			10	10
Resumes after completing one alternative task, then does second alternative task		4	2	6
Resumes after completing both alternative tasks			5	5
Looks at main task before doing alternative task	1			1
Does not complete alternative task; does not resume	1			1
Remarks about incompleteness of main task			1	1
Does one alternative task, part of second, and main task, then finishes alternative task			1	1
Before interruption expresses intention not to finish main task			2	2
Resumes main task after partly completing alternative task	1			1
Remarks about incompleteness of main task, amount still to be done, intention to finish, etc.	1	2		3

Table 11 gives the various responses occurring in subjects who did not resume the main task immediately after the interruption. It may be pointed out here that only four of the subjects showed behavior that could be classified as nonresumption in all three situations; only six showed such behavior in two situations; and the largest number, thirty-two, failed to resume immediately in only one situation. Thus it may be said that, as a general rule, few subjects consistently failed to resume immediately.

It is interesting to note that some of the subjects who failed to resume the interrupted activity showed a *tendency* to go back to the unfinished task.

S brought the sewing to E. "I'll finish the shovel next time."

S talked to E a few seconds, then picked up the sewing. "I'll leave some other children do the rest." He then counted the crayons and left the room.

S brought the paper and crayons to E and asked if he might "put the lights in the Christmas tree" (an alternative task that he had not done in another experiment).

Turning now to the cases of delayed resumption, we note that in some instances, after the subject had completed an alternative task, he expressed a need or desire to finish the interrupted activity.

S went immediately to the alternative task (mosaic) after the interruption. "Now do I try to make this one?" After completing the alternative task, she remarked, "I'm not through with the Easter eggs yet. I have to fix the Easter eggs." She resumed.

S did one of the alternative tasks after the interruption, then finished the main task. "Have to put this in" (matching). She then completed the second alternative task.

S did both alternative tasks, then resumed the main task. "I have to do one more there" (pointing to the uncompleted balloons).

Another interesting type of behavior occurring in subjects who resumed the main task after one or both alternative tasks is illustrated in the following cases:

Before the interruption S remarked, "I'm not going to do all these" (color the balloons). After the interruption he did one of the alternative tasks, then resumed the main task, and finally did the second alternative task.

At the beginning of the main task S said, "I can't do all these holes" (sewing). "I'll do those over there" (alternative tasks). S did both alternative tasks after the interruption. While doing the second one he remarked, "I have to do that yet too" (pointing to the main task). He resumed and completed the interrupted task.

The cases below are of some interest in that they show a type of behavior that one would expect to be characteristic of subjects who resumed immediately. Surprisingly enough, resistance to interruption occurs as frequently in cases of nonresumption as in cases of resumption. Five per cent of each group responded in this way.

S put three more discs into the matching game before E could stop her. "I'll do this first." She went immediately to the alternative task (the basket) after the interruption. After pasting one row of eggs on the basket she resumed the main activity.

S sewed another hole after E had asked him to do the puzzle. After the interruption he asked E if he could draw another man. When E refused to let him do this he left with the remark, "Then I can go." He looked at the main task as he left the room.

V. SUMMARY AND CONCLUSIONS

The purpose of this study was to determine the effect of various factors upon the frequency of resumption of interrupted activities. One hundred and seventy-seven children between the ages of four and one-half years and five and one-half years served as subjects in 486 experiments.

The general procedure was to start the subject at a task and then to interrupt after he had finished a certain proportion of it by giving him another task to perform. After the interruption the subject was free to do as he wished. Three experimental situations were used. In Situation I only the interrupted activity was present; Situation II the interrupted activity and one other activity; and in Situation III the interrupted activity and two other activities. The interruption always occurred either near the beginning, near the middle, near the point where the task was three-fourths complete, or near the end of the task.

The main experimental findings are as follows:

1. Resumption occurs less frequently when the interruption is near the end of the activity than when it is near the beginning, middle, or point of three-fourths completion.

2. There is some tendency for the percentage of resumption to be slightly less when the alternative tasks are present in the situation than when only the interrupted task is present. However, even in situations where the alternative tasks are present, the percentage of resumption remains exceedingly high.

3. The effect of alternative tasks upon the frequency of resumption does not vary with the point of interruption.

4. The nature of the interrupted task affects the frequency with which it is resumed.

5. Within a normal range, the intelligence of the subjects cannot be considered a factor affecting frequency of resumption.

6. Frequency of resumption is not influenced by socio-economic status.

7. Many of the subjects display behavior which, in its qualitative aspects, seems to point to the existence of a tension system related to a need or desire to finish the interrupted activity.

In general, the results of this study confirm the findings of other investigators that interrupted activities tend to be resumed. In the opinion of the writer, Lewin's concept of tension systems is a useful and entirely plausible way of explaining this phenomenon. An important problem that future investigations must consider is whether such tension systems arise because of training or whether they represent an unlearned reaction tendency.

BIBLIOGRAPHY

1. BROWN, J. F. The methods of Kurt Lewin in the psychology of action and affection. Psychological Review, 36: 200-21 (1929).
2. FREEMAN, G. L. Changes in tonus during completed and interrupted mental work. Journal of General Psychology, 4: 309-34 (1930).
3. GOODENOUGH, FLORENCE L. Measurement of intelligence by drawings. World Book Co., Chicago, 1926. 177 pp.
4. LEWIN, K. A dynamic theory of personality. McGraw-Hill Book Co., New York, 1935. 286 pp.
5. ————. Principles of topological psychology. McGraw-Hill Book Co., New York, 1936. 231 pp.
6. LISSNER, KÄTE. Die Entspannung von Bedürfnissen durch Ersatzhandlungen. Psychologische Forschung, 18: 218-50 (1933).
7. McKINNEY, F. Studies in the retention of interrupted learning activities. Journal of Comparative Psychology, 19: 265-96 (1935).
8. MAHLER, WERA. Ersatzhandlungen verschiedenen Realitätsgrades. Psychologische Forschung, 18: 27-89 (1933).
9. OVSIANKINA, MARIA. Die Wiederaufnahme unterbrochener Handlungen. Psychologische Forschung, 11: 302-79 (1928).
10. PACHAURI, A. R. A study of Gestalt problems in completed and interrupted tasks. British Journal of Psychology, 25: 447-57 (1935).
11. ROSENZWEIG, SAUL. The recall of finished and unfinished tasks as affected by the purpose with which they were performed. Psychological Bulletin, 30: 698 (1933).
12. SANDVOSS, H. Uber die Beziehungen von Determination und Bewusstsein bei der Realisierung unerledigter Tätigkeiten. Archiv für die gesamte Psychologie, 89: 139-92 (1933).
13. SCHLOTE, W. Uber die Bevorzugung unvollendeter Handlungen. Zeitschrift für Psychologie, 117: 1-72 (1930).
14. ZEIGARNIK, BLUMA. Das Behalten erledigter und unerledigter Handlungen. Psychologische Forschung, 9: 1-85 (1927).

INDEX

51